PICTURE WINDOW BOOKS
a capstone imprint

Editor: Julie Gassman
Designer: Ashlee Suker
Art Director: Nathan Gassman
Production Specialist: Laura Manthe
The illustrations in this book were created with water color.

Picture Window Books
1710 Roe Crest Drive
North Mankato, MN 56003
www.capstonepub.com

Library of Congress Cataloging-in-Publication Data
Manushkin, Fran.
  Stick to the facts, Katie : writing a research paper with Katie Woo /
by Fran Manushkin ; illustrated by Tammie Lyon.
      p. cm. — (Katie Woo, star writer)
  Includes sidebars with instructions on writing a research paper.
  Summary: Katie's school assignment is to pick a topic and write a
research paper on it, and when she picks butterflies as her subject she
learns that even small animals can be very interesting.
  ISBN 978-1-4048-8130-3 (library binding)
  ISBN 978-1-4795-1925-5 (paperback)
  ISBN 978-1-4795-1891-3 (eBook PDF)
1. Woo, Katie (Fictitious character)—Juvenile fiction. 2. Chinese
Americans—Juvenile fiction. 3. Report writing—Juvenile fiction.
[1.Chinese Americans—Fiction. 2. Report writing—Fiction.] I. Lyon,
Tammie, ill. II. Title.

PZ7.M3195Sti 2013
813.54—dc23   2013004209

Printed in the United States of America in Stevens Point, Wisconsin.
032013   007227WZF13

Katie Woo

Star Writer

Stick to the Facts, Katie

Writing a Research Paper with Katie Woo

by Fran Manushkin

illustrated by Tammie Lyon

Katie was worried.

"What's the matter?" asked JoJo.

"We need to write a

research paper," said

Katie. "But I can't

decide what to

write about."

Katie's Star Tip

What is a research paper? It's a paper that tells you the facts about something. But you can't write your paper until you pick a topic. The topic is what your paper is about. It could be about zebras or airplanes. Or penguins. Or almost anything!

"I'm writing about whales," said

JoJo. "Whales are big and strong.

They are so cool!"

"I'm writing about airplanes," said Pedro. "Planes are powerful! They can fly around the world."

Katie's Star Tip

Brainstorming can help you pick a topic. List animals you like, places you want to visit, or things you want to learn about. Sometimes looking at photos helps you decide. Then pick the idea you like best.

Katie went home and talked to her dad. As they picked tomatoes, a butterfly flew by.

"Butterflies are pretty," said Katie. "I will write about them."

Katie began thinking about butterflies. "I don't know much about them," she said. "I wonder what butterflies do when it snows? They don't have winter coats to wear."

Katie's Star Tip

After you choose your topic, make a list of questions to ask about it. You will answer these in your research paper. I want to know what butterflies do in the winter. I also want to know how far they can fly.

Pedro called Katie. He told her, "I've found lots of neat photos of airplanes. My report will be exciting!"

"Good for you," said Katie. "I hope mine will be exciting too."

Katie's Star Tip

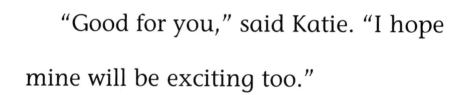

Do you know the most important part of writing a research paper? It's the research! You can find facts about your topic in books and magazines. The internet is good too. But be careful! Some websites don't have correct information. A grown-up can help you pick a website you can trust.

The next day in class, JoJo told

Katie, "Did you know that blue whales

are the biggest animals ever?"

"Wow!" said Katie. "Butterflies are

so small."

Katie began reading about butterflies. She read: "Butterflies lay lots of eggs."

"Guess what?" said JoJo. "Whales have one baby at a time."

"Ha!" said Katie. "Butterflies have hundreds!"

Katie read some more about butterflies: "The butterfly eggs turn into larvae. They look a lot like worms."

"Spaghetti looks like worms too," said Katie.

"But it tastes great!"

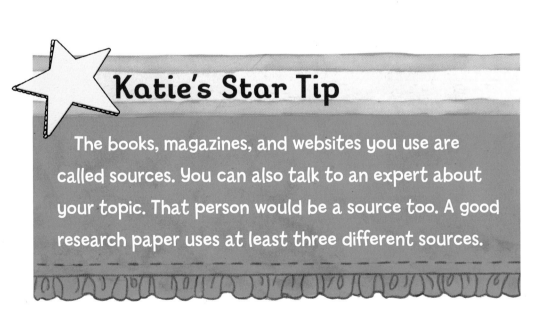

Katie's Star Tip

The books, magazines, and websites you use are called sources. You can also talk to an expert about your topic. That person would be a source too. A good research paper uses at least three different sources.

In class the next day, Katie painted a picture of a butterfly. She told Miss Winkle, "Butterflies are pretty, but they are not exciting. And I still don't know what they do when it snows."

"Keep reading," said Miss Winkle.

"Butterflies are small, but they can do

something big."

Katie looked at the calendar.

"I must write my report soon,"

she said. "But I don't know what

butterflies do that is exciting."

Katie's mom asked, "Do you want
me to tell you what it is?"

"No!" said Katie. "I want to find
out myself."

The next day at school, Katie read some more: "Each butterfly larva turns into a pupa. It looks like a cocoon, but it isn't." Katie wrote that down.

Katie's Star Tip

While you research, you should write down the facts you have found. You can use note cards for this. Here's one way to do it: At the top of each card, write down one of the questions you have about your topic. When you find the answers, you can fill them in.

Katie found out more about butterflies. She read, "It takes ten days to two weeks for a pupa to become a butterfly."

"That's fast," Katie told JoJo. "It will take me years to become a grown-up!"

Katie made notes of what she read. "Butterflies have four stages: egg, larva, pupa, and butterfly."

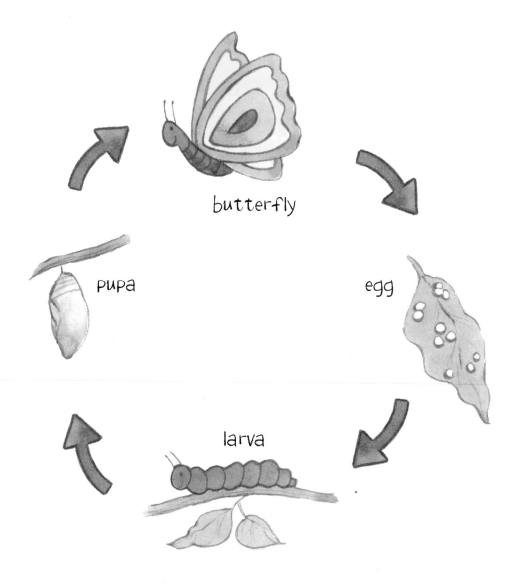

butterfly

egg

pupa

larva

Katie kept finding new facts. She read: "When it rains, butterflies hide under a leaf."

"That's clever," said Katie. "But it's not too exciting. I want my paper to be exciting!"

That night, it snowed. "Brr!" Katie shivered. "I wish I was on a warm beach."

That gave Katie an idea. She told her mom, "Maybe butterflies go somewhere warm when it snows! I will find out!"

Katie and her dad looked it up on the Internet. She read: "Some monarch butterflies migrate south for the winter. They fly more than 2,000 miles to a warmer place."

"Wow!" Katie shouted. "That's a big thing to do! I will put that in my paper."

Katie wrote the first draft of her paper.

She included the three parts

that Miss Winkle talked about: the

introduction, body, and conclusion.

She made some spelling mistakes, but

she could fix them later.

Butrflies are amazing. They hav 4 stages: egg, larva, pupa, and butrfly. Their wings are tinee, but they can fli more than 2,000 miles! Butrflies are powrful. Hurray for butrflies!

Katie's Star Tip

The introduction tells your reader the topic. It can be a sentence or a short paragraph. After that comes the body with all the facts you've found. The last part is the conclusion. It's a sentence or two that gives your reader a final understanding of your topic.

Katie showed her paper to JoJo.

"You left out the part about butterflies hiding under leaves when it rains," said JoJo.

"I will add that," said Katie. "I left out other neat facts too. And I'll fix my spelling mistakes. JoJo, I'm so glad I showed you my paper!"

Katie's Star Tip

Sometimes your paper may need more research and writing. This is called revision. When you revise a paper, you can make it even better. Sometimes your friends can help. JoJo helped me!

The next day, Miss Winkle asked,
"Who would like to read their paper
to the class?"

"Me!" said Katie.

"All right," said Miss Winkle.

Katie began to read:

"Butterflies are amazing! They have four stages: egg, larva, pupa, and butterfly. When it rains, they hide under a leaf. When it snows they fly south where it's warmer. Their wings are tiny, but they can fly 2,000 miles! Butterflies don't have engines like airplanes. They aren't big like whales. But they are powerful. Hurray for butterflies!"

"Well done!" said Miss Winkle!

On the way home, Katie told JoJo and Pedro, "The next paper I'm writing will be about dogs. I'll start by playing with Pedro's dog. That will be fun research."

And it was!

Write a Research Paper!

- It is fun to learn about new things, and when you use your research to write a paper, you can share everything you learn with others. Here are some ideas for research papers:

  - ❀ Choose a city you would like to visit, then research what it is like there. Include specific things you would like to see.

  - ❀ Pick your favorite animal and learn about its life cycle.

  - ❀ What is your favorite holiday? Research the history of that special day.

  - ❀ Research what school is like in another country. What do kids like you learn in France or China or Ghana?

  - ❀ Choose a president, author, or another famous person. Learn facts about his or her life.

Glossary

body—the main part of a written piece

brainstorming—coming up with lots of ideas all at once, without stopping to judge them

conclusion—the final part of a written piece

fact—a piece of information about something

first draft—the first version of a report before revision has taken place

introduction—the first part of a written piece

research—to study a subject in an organized way

research paper—a type of writing that gives information about a topic

revision—changing a piece of writing to make it better

source—a book, article, person, or group that provides information about a topic

topic—a subject or main area of interest

Read More

Fields, Jan. *You Can Write Excellent Reports.* You Can Write. Mankato, Minn.: Capstone Press, 2012.

Lynette, Rachel. *Ben and Bailey Build a Book Report.* Writing Builders. Chicago: Norwood House Press, 2012.

Minden, Cecilia and Kate Roth. *How to Write a Report.* Language Arts Explorer Junior. Ann Arbor, Mich.: Cherry Lake Pub., 2011.

On the Internet

✿ Learn more about Katie and her friends.

✿ Find a Katie Woo color sheet, scrapbook, and stationery.

✿ Discover more Katie Woo books.

All at ... www.capstonekids.com

Still Want More?
Find cool websites related to this book at *www.facthound.com*.

Just type in this code: **9781404881303** and you're ready to go!

About the Author

Fran ManusŠin is the author of many popular picture books, including *Baby, Come Out!*; *Latkes and Applesauce: A Hanukkah Story*; *The Tushy Book*; *The Belly Book*; and *Big Girl Panties*. There is a real Katie Woo—she's Fran's great-niece—but she never gets in half the trouble of the Katie Woo in the books. Fran writes on her beloved Mac computer in New York City, without the help of her two naughty cats, Chaim and Goldy.

About the Illustrator

Tammie Lyon began her love for drawing at a young age while sitting at the kitchen table with her dad. She continued her love of art and eventually attended the Columbus College of Art and Design, where she earned a bachelor's degree in fine art. Today she lives with her husband, Lee, in Cincinnati, Ohio. Her dogs, Gus and Dudley, keep her company as she works in her studio.

Look for all the books in the series:

It Doesn't Need to Rhyme, Katie

Sincerely, Katie

Stick to the Facts, Katie

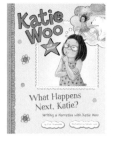

What Do You Think, Katie?

What Happens Next, Katie?

What's in Your Heart, Katie?